cuntstruck

poems

Kate Northrop

C&R Press
Conscious & Responsible

Summer Tide Pool Chapbook
2016 Second Selection 1 of 3   CB3

Cover Art and Design by Sally Underwood
Interior Layout and Design by Liz Harms

ISBN: 978-1-936196-72-2

C&R Press
Conscious & Responsible
www.crpress.org

For special discounted bulk purchases please contact:
C&R Press sales@crpress.org

cuntstruck

CONTENTS

In the Snow

Now there's a man in the distance
And you are driving the car

Now he is in the distance
No bag beside him no car

And you see he is complete
As a knock as a dog's bark

But belonging only to himself
In the empty road in the snow

Now there's a man in the distance
And you are driving the car

High Plains
(overnight, at 40 below)

The town drawn in and quiet, as the inside
Of a closet. Impenetrable as a dream

But still the interstate slides by

The semis rising from the east,
Outlined in lights, all lighted up!

And dropping into the valley again
Goodbye: they drop

Easily as coins through a broken soda machine

(easily as snow-crust struck by sun: someone I loved once
Opening the curtain and flushed, I remember in the mirror,
Mint-bright, fuck-stunned)

And they drop away from us, from our houses
Facing the prairie

Which we see tonight
As if on the brink: still, moon-white.

Decorations

Ghosts have been tied into the trees.
At dawn they pivot
In the wind slowly.

Where the moon windows in
I am of those
Who can't stand it

Kept awake, humming with trucks
While anything lunar
Won't rut, ruminates. Overhead, *uh-hunh*—

What is a ghost? What's *poetry?*
And time? *Time needs no hanky, time blows by*
the Kleenex flowers. Or time's

so slow, starry-cold, even is cold
            and sure, little admonishments.

                    •

Were you awake all night?

I was. I was awake all night.

The Apartment

Remember the Worcester apartment: third floor
    of a three-family, in the upper reaches of the elms. Whole afternoons
could still in it, each room

oddly bright inside, like the bloom at the top of a hollyhock.

          •

I remember the apartment, third floor
    "like a tree-house" but the layout
forcing a passage, a certain

loop: entering into the living room, you turned

right through an arch into the dining room, and then again
through another, smaller arch

into the kitchen at the back, crammed in
under crooked eaves. Plotted like a child's story *(and just then--)* each room

offered a second door, a way onward: through the kitchen
into the bedroom, through bedroom into the long

paneled hall, which ended, at the front door again. Afternoons
    you could sit

in the filtered light, obliterating
as a perfect argument. Or watch the leaves rustle, but it was too weird,
being up there, eventually

like being a breath. Like being only the thought

your mind was having.

•

The rain thumps against the house. It thumps
on the side of the house. Thumps against it—

In a thicket, a rabbit blinks. That is to say,
in the pause before a boat responds—

I remember your apartment, more peculiar
by night (the candles

only worsened it, a flame disappearing in the apartment's distance, then
    reappearing,
like a fire at the far end of a field) and I moved through quietly

in circulation, except
there was nothing at the center, there was

no center there at all, only

the sound of you, turning over, and a car door
    slammed below. Often in those moments

I imagined the children. And now they are beautiful, stretched on the floor, chins in their little, perfect hands.   Now they are watching

    a huge, speckled TV—   silver TV

          •

And Love, I hear you, but I am tired (so tired!) of sky that comes down in snow

There must be something to believe

But I know there is nothing to believe

The Field the Drive-In Was In

        —what are we here? The hive mind
answers hive-ily, and the suggestions
make for us, make for us: *brzoom*, as
high school boys, cunt-struck.

"Oh we were young, oh we banged around the world,
holding our arms out, hoping for what?"

All the while, something, my love, bore down on the boat, a power
quick and sickly, cut-throat.
But we happened,

we happened, drawing each other out,
reading newspapers and novels until the marina
swooped back into view.

Across the water, shimmering:
powerful, calming, and regular as credits—

Yellow Cup

On the kitchen counter, it rings the counter
And the sound wakes…what? Wakes the kitchen,
Tremulous, arranged suddenly, as if on a string.

But sometimes the call goes out and all that returns
Is some bumper-sticker: *Easy Does It*

Anyhoo, when you return you will see
How the dishes settle under the dishwater,
Clunking like dull mollusks

How the sky comes down
and greens the window

So when Charles told me, *I am brokenhearted*

Charlie, I said, wean yourself from love-bunk!
And it's no joke, no joke: these days

I must draw myself
From uncertain sights: the neighbor's dog

in the middle of the pond, in the middle of the night.

You, Don Draper

Headlights' beams from the 1970s, you pass over a wood-paneled wall

•

At your window, you look far off

Like rocks on the side of the road, your face
facets back the light

when a woman enters the room. (I like entering rooms, I do, but being
    female
is withheld. I must leap for it, leap.) Draper,

at the root of love for you, sheets of ice
shift and clatter,

old men groan. At the root
is a blizzard into the city, driving whiteness at the root, is my uncle
on his apartment floor, overdosed. Christmas,

1975. The holidays
ring along, skaters ring. Skaters! In the distance, Jim O'Brien
dives over our house

then is a broken body, at United Parachute. Jim O'Brien,

the newscaster, earnestly mustached, our caster of kernels of news

11

Jubilee Days

This fair's a total fuck-up. At it,
feelings drift in the straw-struck heat.

We're prickled with itch
and the slumped-over girl
studies strands of her hair. *Holy Moly!*

mouths the avuncular Ferris Wheel, its face
a big, fat barn. Beyond the field
is a burnt-out creek. There are feelings

moving about the world: urgent,
anadromous. At the Scrambler, the
attendant's eyes

won't resolve, floating
ghosts of themselves, weird as fireflies

The Roof-Runners
(in the city, at night)

I. *from underneath*

Exactly what they are's unclear, but we wake

already listening. *The fuck*
        was that? We develop
some understanding slowly, their footsteps

still drifting through, like algae in a shaft of light

and their laughter carried off   beyond us, coherent,
a sentence in a dream. In the morning, sure,

we know we know them. *Those fucking kids—*
and we hurtle

into our work day: *then I said* and *you know me!*

13

II. *outside*

In August for four nights, maybe five

In August for four or five nights
going over the row-homes on Ogden,

and afterwards, startled by something, a premonition,
like entering a room
where the window's been left open

          •

But daylight draws things
back to the world, lines and suspends them

     —greasy slats
in a blind, a stop-sign—   until they hum

brilliantly, like light bulbs,
the chain swinging in a darkened room, beside a light bulb.

.

Giraffe

(in Wyoming)

Out of chicken wire and weather,
it appears on the neighbors' lawn

•

It's simple: the water they spilled over
freezes there
into sheet and icicle   —and the dumb bumps
my hand wants.

Now we walk by. Now evening
arrogates a giraffe, its eyes
cold as a light on the surface of a lake.

Vatic giraffe! ...if you could gallop savannah,
you would sound like holidays
in our rickety, old apartments

but you are clear as these days
and brutal truthful, like pattern. Someone
passed out on a carpet—   flat—

I know the neighbors who imagined you
already have dismantled you, piece
by funny piece.

Decompression Hang

The boat was floating overhead

and so the world would alternate. In shade,
then full in the sun she felt

her body'd been remembered   ideally, sweetly

The Man on my Roof
(California, early in the morning)

Hey, my neighbor calls up, *Hey Man!* His voice
Makes straight for the roof—

But who squats on my roof, arms
Around his knees, stares at the roof

Like a boy in a small field, lighting a fire.

•

And however early sunlight
Covers my bungalow   with streets, pollen, shrubs

The police arrive directly, arranging themselves
Around the dream of the squad car. *Let's quit
Dicking around*   someone says.

The man lifts his head.

He shakes his head, a little sadly,
And holds one hand up, like someone
Who is sorry, he must interrupt—

But he won't look at us, as the sun
Rises beyond us

And horns & stereos also rise   until *whoosh,*
The morning's kaput and day assembles

Into sheet music, storefronts. (The world you know

Will not meet, although the slanted rooftops
Flash, immediately in the light. Gleaming,

They darken, like large sea-rocks.)

The Picture Window

Rises nightly over the dark street

Withdraws, or begins to, the blue-black

Held loosely, like a boat
Against which the grasses

Froth up.

              You, Willie, never mind.

      •

Inside: the gray stalks of hollyhocks
Knock against the glass (such a *movement* to the boat, a tree
Grown through it)

But you know this space isn't a hallway.

It isn't a hallway
And the boat presses in, coldly imposing.

Tell me.

No, no, no, no, no.

      •

And then:

Rain of brittle aspen leaves.

•

Some cocksucker, Jesus Christ,
      some little motherfucker—

Some Mirrors, We Don't Appear

The sunlight showers like children through a playground
and still we feel wretched,

pocked, like the bottom of homemade bread, duly watched—

What's to remember? Five or six tents
glowing along the edge of the meadow

and in the morning, the dew
moved there without moving, like the sea—

Outside are two women walking by

Sugar, one says, *it's the devil!*   and her voice hangs in the air, tilts
like an old signpost in a photo. Sugar
really *is* the devil

and I see I am going to have to work all night,

going to have to knock on your breastbone, *Hello, Ocean?*
knock on your noggin'. *Hello? Hello?*

But what happens is this: in the morning we walk

around and around, trying to find a way in.

In the Old Army Navy
(9th and Chestnut)

The elevator, "claptrap" he'd said,
was right at the back of the jacket aisle.
A clerk took us up—

swung the door open where it soared, the old gym
qua tent room, white and stripped
into us: the high windows

waved and stained, the bleachers
bright and dusty, and across the hardwood floor
dozens of erected tents (dark red, orange, one

a yellow-green) in the fans, fluttering
in the fans a little.

·

The clerk cleared her throat. *You can go in.*

She sneezed into her sleeve,
then we were climbing in the tents like children,
on our hands and knees.

Hush Flares

1.

At the end is Heathcliff's body
rigid in the drenching rain,

like a swimming pool glowing at night.

2.

        (the crappy elevator)

Going out, it goes like this: surely I did,

lock the apartment, and I see
that movement in memory.   Something, a party

has drawn us. It draws us
staring at the ceiling of the elevator—

And reading graffiti, *where's my money Jerry?* noticing chipped paint's
dark, industrial grade

lead nowhere. Wrappers, from the deli
at the corner, shift into corners.

It's gotten icy out. Easy now.

.

Hey Buttercup

They form yellow meadows
Away you go
and dazzle the sunshine

Water Crowfoot, Lesser Celandine

They call, window to window
Can't let go
and flash, like blades of scissors

They get so tired, swimming all night,
turning circles under the moon-spill
All things being equal

and in the morning, look again:
here's your meadow,
here's your yellow meadow

Decompression Hang

The boat was floating overhead

and so the world would alternate. In shade,
then full in the sun she felt

her body'd been remembered   ideally, sweetly

Where her toes were went down, the cold
forming, reforming, those voices

one will never hear again, but hears.   *It's morning*—

And fish she'd never seen, how a school's

a cloud, dimly dreamt, all atmosphere
then flashed back into a chorus line—

Weekends We Spent
(upstate)

I used to call him Miss B, never mind why.
The piano hulked through winter, holding down the room—
It had the look of someone crossing a field.

When Miss B pissed in the middle of the night, I listened in
—on viewless wings! and the sound
lingered in the dark, like airplane wreckage

long exploded in some woods. Poor kitchen,
creaking beneath. Poor falling-down
house across the road, held up years

in escaping collapse, open to headlights, cans,
drifts of snow. At four a.m., where Miss B went?
He'd read, or write   ....footsteps moving below

from room to room, like a history class,
but once when he said *what happened to you*
didn't I hate his bones & guts? And hate

the age? Everyone wanted to eat,
then arrange their feelings. When I went out
before dawn, I'd walk the road, past Shevick's

field, where cows were breathing, some
appearing almost at the fence, their bodies big
and blank, like shades pulled down.

Some things look, in daylight, like broken bones

A stepladder in the grass, the curtain
in a window. "You should have known
to be here on time"   was strange reprimand to us,

who had no way of knowing, and still
when mail arrived, we drew in from the edges
like the circle of foam

around a dripping storm drain. Had we been warned
we might not have left our homes
for a day so much had fallen from:

I found a single hoof, half-buried
in the sand, and so small
it must have belonged to a fawn.

Surely we'd have stayed in
through evening, the walls' plaster
cool as a passage, the walls

moving our neighbors' lives
—smell of food frying, TV racket   into our lives
where they can never end

•

(But sometimes, when we think we are ready,
light mildens, and the animals come to us:
        Biscuit, Willie, Jester, Sparkle-Mousse.)

She was loose-limbed

like stuff in the back of a truck
going over a bump. When she sat reading
she was green and quiet,

distinct at first, then blurred
like a paper napkin's grease. *What time is it?*
seemed to be a question

novels asked. The evening
fell like a bird, fell so fast
we could just remember, how it felt

fucking and getting fucked, how we lingered
smoking in the dark outside
but never heard the tall

tree in the ear! Heard only
our own breath, a dull scuffling
like the sound ballet shoes make

during the ballet. The notes
stuck in our throat? The body
stormed to stay alive? We know

she studied her options,
like us. Like us, she stood
days at the window, the wail of sirens

banging off the city walls—
Then walked out into sun? So bright
it was like walking

into someone else's applause?
A force as fierce as roses
climbing over a gate.

after (far after) Chang-rae Lee's *On Such a Full Sea*

ACKNOWLEDGMENTS

I am grateful to the editors of the following journals and projects, in which some of these poems first appeared: *The Academy of American Poets Poem-A-Day series, AGNI, The American Poetry Review, Locomotive, New South, Plume, The Plume Anthology of Poetry 5, Poetry Congeries, Raritan, Tamsen,* and *The Virginia Quarterly Review.* I'm grateful to Peter Behrens for featuring some of these poems on his blog, *Autoliterate.* I'm also grateful to Caldera, the MacDowell Colony and Yaddo for supporting the making of this work.

My many thanks to Alyson Hagy, Nell Hanley, Jane Hilberry, Beth Loffreda and especially and always to Harvey.

Some echoes in this collection: Rilke's tall tree in the ear, Keats' viewless wings, and Lucinda Williams' *Can't Let Go.*

C&R PRESS CHAPBOOKS

C&R Press hosts two chapbook selection periods from June to September and November to March coupled with a reading in New York City each year. The Winter Soup Bowl and Summer Tide Pool Chapbook Series are open to new and established writers in poetry, fiction, essay and other creative writing.

2016 SUMMER TIDE POOL SELECTIONS

Cuntstruck
by Kate Northrop

Relief Map
by Erin M. Bertram

Love Undefined
by Jonathan Katz

2016 Winter Soup Bowl

Notes from the Negro Side of the Moon
by Earl Braggs

A Hunger Called Music: A Verse History in Black Music
by Meredith Nnoka

OTHER C&R PRESS TITLES

FICTION

Ivy vs. Dogg
by Brian Leung

A History of the Cat In Nine Chapters or Less
by Anis Shivani

While You Were Gone
by Sybil Baker

Spectrum
by Martin Ott

That Man in Our Lives
by Xu Xi

SHORT FICTION

Meditations on the Mother Tongue
by An Tran

The Protester Has Been Released
by Janet Sarbanes

ESSAY AND CREATIVE NONFICTION

Immigration Essays
by Sybil Baker

Je suis l'autre: Essays and Interrogations
by Kristina Marie Darling

Death of Art
by Chris Campanioni

POETRY

Negro Side of the Moon
by Early Braggs

Holdfast
by Christian Anton Gerard

Ex Domestica
by E.G. Cunningham

Collected Lies and Love Poems
by John Reed

Imagine Not Drowning
by Kelli Allen

Les Fauves
by Barbara Crooker

Tall as You are Tall Between Them
by Annie Christain

The Couple Who Fell to Earth
by Michelle Bitting

www.ingramcontent.com/pod-product-compliance
Lightning Source LLC
Chambersburg PA
CBHW032107040426
42449CB00007B/1212